KING'S COLLEGE LONDON
CENTRE FOR LATE ANTIQUE & MEDIEVAL STUDIES
OCCASIONAL PUBLICATIONS, 1

LIFTING THE VEIL:
SEXUAL/TEXTUAL NAKEDNESS IN THE
ROMAN DE LA ROSE

Alastair J. Minnis

KING'S COLLEGE LONDON
CENTRE FOR LATE ANTIQUE & MEDIEVAL STUDIES
1995

© Alastair J. Minnis 1995

ISSN 1360-385X

ISBN 0 9522119 1 2

Printed in England on acid-free paper

by

Short Run Press Ltd

Exeter

1993

PREFACE

The Centre for Late Antique and Medieval Studies (CLAMS) was founded at King's College London in 1988. Since 1992 it has been closely linked with the Centres for Advanced Musical Studies, Hellenic Studies, Philosophical Studies, American Studies, and Twentieth-century Cultural Studies within the academic and administrative setting provided by the Humanities Research Centres (HRC). The range of subject interests covered by CLAMS and the chronological span of the period between Late Antiquity and the end of the Middle Ages make it unique in Britain, while its juxtaposition with the Centre for Hellenic Studies makes for a combination of Eastern and Western Medieval Studies that is extremely rare anywhere and without obvious parallel in this country. The Centre was established in order to realize the benefits of increased co-operation among specialists in the many fields concerned, both in teaching and in research. It includes among its members experts in Late Antique and Byzantine Studies, medieval languages and literatures (Old English, Middle English, Old French, Old and Middle High German, Old Icelandic, medieval Greek, Latin, Portuguese and Spanish), Palaeography and codicology, Germanic and Romance philology, medieval History, Music, Philosophy, Theology, and Warfare.

CLAMS has established itself as an international centre for the study of medieval life and culture *inter alia* by the organisation of a series of triennial international conferences. The first of these took place in April, 1992. The proceedings, *Kings and Kingship in Medieval Europe*, edited by the organizer, Dr Anne Duggan, appeared at the end of 1993 as volume 10 of the series King's College London Medieval Studies, which is published in association with CLAMS. The second conference, on the complementary theme

'Queens and Queenship in Medieval Europe', was held in April, 1995. Its proceedings are likewise to be published. Interspersed among these large-scale international events have been day-colloquia held each December. Topics thus far have been: 'Richard the Lionheart' (1989), 'Medieval Marriage and Divorce' (1990), 'War and Peace in the Middle Ages' (1991), 'Sickness and Health in the Middle Ages' (1992), 'Outsiders and Aliens in Medieval Societies' (1993), and 'Parents and Children in Medieval Societies' (1994).

The Centre's annual programme of public lectures, which extends throughout the academic year, has featured many distinguished speakers, and has become a staging post for foreign scholars visiting this country. From 1992-1993, by arrangement with Professor A.C. de la Mare, the Annual Special Palaeography Lecture of the University of London has been associated with the Centre, commencing with that delivered in June 1993 before many authorities in the field by Professor Mirella Ferrari of the Catholic University of Milan, and entitled 'Circulation of Books and Libraries in Lombardic Italy'. The previous month had seen the first Public Lecture in the special annual series inaugurated by the Centre itself, when Professor Christopher Brooke (University of Cambridge) addressed a crowded audience on 'Bede as Historian'. Since his material was conceived as an integral part of a larger whole, it was not available for publication in separate form.

It is for this reason that the present lecture, the first in the annual series to be printed, is that delivered in June 1994 by Professor Alastair Minnis of the Centre for Medieval Studies, University of York. In his lecture ('Lifting the Veil: Sexual/Textual Nakedness in the *Roman de la Rose*') Professor Minnis accepts that Jean de Meun, in his portion of the *Roman*, displays a command of the 'integumental' method of interpretation, which detects and seeks to unveil layers of allegorical meaning beneath the literal surface of the 'playful fables' of the classical poets. But the principal characteristic of Jean de Meun's approach, Professor Minnis argues, arises from his affinity with satirists such as Juvenal, so that, even where the theory of love is concerned, he is a friend of open, indeed 'naked' speech, which has no truck with obscuring integument, either at the level of language or of poetic invention. Apart from the elegance and subtlety of its argument, this lecture triumphantly satisfies the rhetorical condition of appropriateness to its purpose. In exploring Jean de Meun's literary intentions it is simply not an option to ignore his relationship—whether direct, or mediated by his twelfth-century predecessors, or by his schooling—to the late classical mythographers, to the Roman satirists, to Ovid in his various modes, or to Boethius. In short, Professor Minnis has furnished us with a striking example of the influence of the late classical tradition, and of its renewal and creative transformation by successive generations of medieval writers, each working within a distinctive set of circumstances, intellectual, social, and artistic. The Centre for Late Antique and Medieval Studies owes its foundation and development precisely to a belief in the lasting interest and importance of such studies, so well represented on the literary front by the work of Professor Minnis.

Finally, at another level of continuity within change, it is a pleasure to acknowledge the contribution made to the production of this series by the desk-top publishing and design skills of Wendy Pank, from the scriptorium of the Humanities Research Centres at King's College London.

R.A. WISBEY
Director, Centre for Late Antique and
Medieval Studies (1988-1994)

LIFTING THE VEIL:
SEXUAL/TEXTUAL NAKEDNESS IN THE
ROMAN DE LA ROSE

'An open and naked exposition of herself (*apertam nudamque expositionem sui*) is distasteful to Nature', declares Macrobius, in explaining why certain philosophers make use of 'fabulous narratives'. Just as Nature 'has withheld an understanding of herself from the vulgar senses of men by enveloping herself in variegated garments', he continues, she 'has also desired to have her secrets handled by more prudent individuals through fabulous narratives'. Thus, 'her sacred rites are veiled in mysterious representations so that she may not have to show herself naked even to initiates. Only eminent men of superior intelligence gain a revelation of her truths [...]'.[1]

In the Twelfth-Century Renaissance various eminent men of superior intelligence, including Bernard of Chartres, William of Conches, and Bernard Silvester, set about widening the Macrobian category of fables which merited the approval of philosophers,[2]

---

[1] Macrobius, *In somnium Scipionis*, ed. by J. Willis, 2nd edn (Leipzig: Teubner, 1970), I.ii.17-18; trans. by W.H. Stahl, *Commentary on the Dream of Scipio by Macrobius* (New York and Oxford, 1952; repr. 1990), pp. 86-87. When expounding this passage in his commentary on Macrobius, William of Conches explains 'naked' as 'that is, without an *integumentum*' and claims that 'only the wise should know the secrets of the gods, (arrived at) through the interpretation of *integumenta*. As for churls and foolish men, let them not know but only believe'. Cited by Peter Dronke, *Fabula. Explorations into the Uses of Myth in Medieval Platonism* (Leiden, 1974), p. 48.

[2] On this widening process see *Medieval Literary Theory and Criticism c.1100-c.1375: The Commentary Tradition*, ed. by A.J. Minnis and A.B. Scott, rev. ed. (Oxford, 1991), p. 119. Here I illustrate how William of Conches was prepared to find scientific truths in fables which Macrobius would probably have dismissed as base and unworthy (cf. *In somn. Scip.*, I.ii.11) with William's integumental reading of the castration of Saturn. See further Dronke's excellent discussion, *Fabula*, pp. 25-30.

through a process of 'integumental' interpretation whereby the veils or garments of allegory were judged to clothe profound truths relating to physics or ethics.[3] In the *Aeneid* commentary sometimes attributed to Bernard it is claimed that Virgil was both a poet and a philosopher, the latter because of his integumental discourse,[4] and a few generations after these scholars flourished, Arnulf of Orléans (*fl.* 1175) extrapolated from Ovid's *Metamorphoses* a series of *allegoriae* which were to enjoy considerable popularity.[5] Moreover, in his *Anticlaudianus* and *De planctu naturae* Alan of Lille (*c.*1116-1202/3) put integumental theory into literary practice. Here, as Alan said of the *Anticlaudianus*, 'the sweetness of the literal sense' is meant to soothe the ears of boys, while 'the moral instruction' will 'inspire the mind on the road to perfection'. Most important and elevated of all, however, is 'the sharper subtlety of the allegory', which is designed to 'whet the advanced intellect'.[6]

The use, or lack of it, which is made of such garments of style in a later text which is highly indebted to *De planctu naturae*, namely Jean de Meun's portion of the *Roman de la Rose* (composed *c.*1269-78), is at the centre of this present paper. The stylistic differences between the two works could hardly be greater. Alan's ornate and

---

[3] For a working definition of the term *integumentum*, which basically means a garment or covering, we need look no further than the prologue to the 'Bernard Silvester' *Aeneid* commentary. There it is explained that the 'integument is a kind of teaching which wraps up the true meaning inside a fictitious narrative (*narratio fabulosa*), and so it is also called "a veil" (*involucrum*)'. See Minnis and Scott, *Medieval Literary Theory*, p. 152.

[4] Minnis and Scott, *Medieval Literary Theory*, p. 150. The argument that this commentary is not the work of Bernard but rather of English origin is included in the study by C. Baswell, 'The Medieval Allegorization of the *Aeneid*: MS Cambridge, Peterhouse 158', *Traditio*, 41 (1985), 181-237.

[5] The main study of Arnulf as Ovid commentator remains F. Ghisalberti, 'Arnolfo d'Orléans, un cultore di Ovidio nel secolo XII', *Memorie del Reale Istituto lombardo di scienze e lettere*, 24.4 (1932), 157-234. See further Frank T. Coulson, 'New Manuscript Evidence for Sources of the *Accessus* of Arnoul d'Orléans to the *Metamorphoses* of Ovid', *Manuscripta*, 30 (1986), 103-07. Arnulf's *allegoriae* were drawn on by the compiler of the major thirteenth-century 'Vulgate' commentary on the *Metamorphoses*, on which see *The 'Vulgate' Commentary on Ovid's 'Metamorphoses': The Creation Myth and the Story of Orpheus*, ed. by Frank T. Coulson (Toronto, 1991); also Coulson's article 'The "Vulgate" Commentary on Ovid's *Metamorphoses*', *Mediaevalia*, 13 (1987), 29-61.

[6] Alan of Lille, *Anticlaudianus*, trans. by J.J. Sheridan (Toronto, 1973), p. 40.

richly artificial *modus loquendi*, with its dazzling rhetoric, convoluted allegory and heavy dependence on classical myth and grammatical metaphors, distances the reader from empirical reality and *temporalia*. And the reader presupposed by *De planctu naturae* is a privileged individual indeed; the knowledge required for comprehension of this text in its entirety, for appreciation of its donnish innuendoes as much as its profoundly learned allusions, ensures that it will remain caviar to the general.[7] In this case Dame Nature need not worry about being exposed to the uninitiated; her secrets remain safe within a clerical coterie. Jean de Meun, however, sought to tell tales out of school (to some extent at least). His 'mirror for lovers' was very much a product of the age which fostered the *Speculum maius* of Vincent of Beauvais, a formidable compilation which boasts (for example) 171 chapters on herbs, 134 chapters on seeds and grains, 161 chapters on birds, and 46 chapters on fishes, all written in a straightforward Latin prose which eschews ambivalence and artifice. While in *De planctu naturae* the book of Nature was 'an infinite book of secrecy',[8] in the *Speculum naturale* Nature's secrets are being inventoried one by one, divided and conquered by scholastic *divisio* and *distinctio*. And Jean's *Speculum amantis* shares some of the formal techniques of the thirteenth-century *compilatio*. *Nuda natura*—for thus may Jean's construct be regarded—describes directly and clearly her own creation, planetary motions and powers, destiny and free will (following Boethius), the influence of the heavens, the properties of mirrors and glasses, dreams and frenzies, and true gentility, concluding with a commendation of all creation, man excepted, for its ordered obedience.

In short, an ornate, richly artificial high style has been made 'plain and open', to adopt a phrase from a typical description of the kind of translation which Jean de Meun is sometimes said to have practised in *Li Livres de confort*, his French rendering of *De*

---

[7] On those donnish innuendoes see especially Jan Ziolkowski, *Alan of Lille's Grammar of Sex: The Meaning of Grammar to a Twelfth-Century Intellectual* (Cambridge, Mass., 1985).
[8] To borrow a phrase from F.J.E. Raby, 'Nuda Natura and Twelfth-Century Cosmology', *Speculum*, 43 (1968), 73-78 (p. 77).

consolatione philosophiae.[9] Jean was a plain-style poet whose main (though by no means only) modes of procedure are narration and exemplification rather than enigmatic fable and allegory ('personification allegory' or prosopopoeia being, of course, a different thing altogether, and fundamental to the poem).[10] The language of the *Rose* is usually outspoken, explicit, literal.

That statement is a controversial one for me to make, however, given that John Fleming has objected to an earlier remark of mine to the effect that Jean de Meun's text generally evinces an attitude which is 'unflinchingly literal'.[11] Jean's theory of love, I went on to say, is expressed in perfectly literal terms. Here I was seeking to align myself with H.R. Jauss, who had suggested that in the *Rose* Jean de Meun no longer took seriously the allegorical mode which he inherited from Alan of Lille,[12] and with Winthrop Wetherbee, who had elaborated that point in the following statement, with which I still warmly concur:

> Certainly the effect of his [i.e. Jean's] allusive dialogue with Alain and the *De Planctu* is to prohibit any naive attempt to educe a higher *significatio* from the facts of human behaviour by resource to the sort of poetic typology which unifies the former poem, realigning its imagery and cosmology with the archetypal pattern which man's depravity had obscured. Raison cites Plato and seeks recourse to *integumanz* in defence of her plain speaking on sexual matters, but the unflinching literalism of la

---

[9] On the style of *Li Livres de Confort* see A.J. Minnis and T.W. Machan, 'The *Boece* as Late-Medieval Translation', in *Chaucer's 'Boece' and the Medieval Tradition of Boethius*, ed. by A.J. Minnis (Cambridge, 1993), pp. 167-88 (pp. 172-73).

[10] Good working definitions of allegory (*not* prosopopoeia) and exemplification are offered in John Burrow's cogent remarks: 'These two modes often overlap in practice, but in theory there is a fundamental distinction between them. Exemplification treats facts or events (real or imagined) as examples which demonstrate some general truth; whereas allegory treats facts or events as metaphors which represent some truth or some other event. Allegory requires the reader to translate; exemplification requires him to generalize'. In *Medieval Writers and their Work. Middle English Literature and its Background 1100-1500* (Oxford, 1982), p. 87.

[11] A.J. Minnis, *Chaucer and Pagan Antiquity* (Cambridge, 1982), p. 16.

[12] H.R. Jauss, 'La Transformation de la forme allégorique entre 1180 et 1240: d'Alain de Lille à Guillaume de Lorris', in *L'Humanisme médiéval dans les littératures romanes*, Centre de philologie et de littératures romanes de l'Université de Strasbourg, Actes et colloques, 3 (Paris, 1964), pp. 107-46.

Vieille and Genius dominates, and reveals how thoroughly Jean has 'de-allegorized' his materials.[13]

Fleming retorts by reiterating the fundamental principle which informs his 1969 and 1984 monographs on the *Rose*: that Jean de Meun expects his audience (an extraordinarily consistent and consensual interpretative community, according to Fleming) to decode the classical fables within his text with the aid of the moral allegories transmitted by the Latin mythographic tradition.[14] It is emphasized that the lover's winning of the Rose is described not literally but obliquely through (*inter alia*) the imagery of a pilgrim worshipping at the shrine of his beloved saint and (with the aid of his stiff and stout staff) entering into her pudendal sanctuary—an allegory which, in Fleming's view, presents Amant's cupidinous behaviour as contemptible idolatry.

But of course, neither Jauss, Wetherbee nor myself would or could deny that Jean sometimes drew on mythographic materials and displayed an awareness of the allegorical or 'integumental' method of interpreting them, and I can safely say that none of us would dream of confusing a pilgrim's staff with a penis. What is at stake here is rather the overall situation of such moves within the text, the status and significance which Jean is affording them within his total project. That is the issue which will now be addressed, in considering the positioning and contestation of literary-theoretical discourses within the *Rose*.

Competing theoretical discourses: allegorical covering *versus* satiric stripping

At one point in the *Rose* Jean de Meun quite unmistakably uses the language of integumental hermeneutics. His character Raison declares that in the *integumanz aus poetes* one will 'see a large part of the secrets of philosophy' (7137-40). Trained clerics have access

---

[13] Winthrop Wetherbee, 'The Literal and the Allegorical: Jean de Meun and the "De Planctu Naturae"', *Mediaeval Studies*, 33 (1971), 264-91 (p. 286).
[14] John V. Fleming, 'Jean de Meun and the Ancient Poets', in *Rethinking the 'Romance of the Rose': Text, Image, Reception*, ed. by Kevin Brownlee and Sylvia Huot (Philadelphia, 1992), pp. 81-100. Cf. Fleming's two monographs, *The 'Roman de la Rose': A Study in Allegory and Iconography* (Princeton, N.J., 1969), and *Reason and the Lover* (Princeton, N.J., 1984).

to those secrets. 'In our schools', she declares, many things are said *par paraboles* which are very beautiful to hear; however, one should not take them *a la letre* (7121-27). The 'playful fables of the poets' in particular offer 'very profitable delights beneath which they cover their thoughts when they clothe the truth in fables' (7145-48).[15]

Here Raison is referring back a long way, to her version of the fable of how Saturn was castrated by his son Jupiter, the result of which was the birth of Venus (5505-12). In this typical case, she assures us, 'The truth hidden within would be clear if it were explained' (7135-36). But the promised exposition is not being provided here (I mean, in Raison's disquisition on *integumanz*). Instead Raison reiterates the point that certain words she had used earlier should be taken 'according to the letter, without gloss' (7151-54). This alludes to Raison's infamous reference to Saturn's balls (*coilles*, 5507): according to her forceful argument she is perfectly justified in naming such noble things (noble because made by God) in plain text, without need of gloss. Glossing is again rejected just before Raison launches into her praise of the integuments of the poets, as cited above. You want me to gloss, she tells Amant scornfully (7052), but why shouldn't I name such parts of the human anatomy directly or 'properly' (*proprement*), i.e. in language which is precise and appropriate, special to the things thereby designated (7095-96, cf. 7049)? Are they not the works of my Father? In sum, here—at the very (and only) point in the entire text at which integumental allegoresis is described, and immediately before the passage which modern panallegorizers regularly cite in justification of their totalizing readings—is a defence of 'proper' language and plain speaking which seems to be quite at variance with the language which values secrecy and concealment and is redolent of the coterie knowledge of the privileged few who have studied long in the schools. Surely passages such as the following may appropriately be described as 'unflinchingly literal':

---

[15] I have used the edition of the *Roman de la Rose* by Félix Lecoy (Paris, 1965-70), and drawn on the translation (though with some alterations) by Charles Dahlberg (Hanover and London, 1971; repr. 1983).

> cui [i.e. Saturnus] Jupiter coupa les coilles,
> ses filz, con se fussent andoilles,
> (mout ot ci dur filz et amer)
> puis les gita dedanz la mer [...]
>
> (5507-10)

[... Saturn, whose balls Jupiter, his hard and bitter son, cut off as though they were sausages and threw into the sea ...]

> Coilles est biaus nons et si l'ains,
> si sunt par foi coillon et vit [...]
>
> (7086-87)

['Balls' is a good name and I like it, and so, in faith, are 'testes' and 'penis'...]

Indeed, there are several distinct but related theoretical discourses functioning within the *Rose* which justify language that is direct, plain and open. One turns on the technical distinction between 'proper' and 'improper' speech, another on the relationship between words and deeds; yet another celebrates a style which presents truth as standing naked, stripped of the veils which conceal the harsh facts of human folly and depravity. Time permits consideration of only one of these: the last discourse here summarised, which defines the objectives of the medieval literary theory of satire.

The Roman satirists, Horace, Juvenal and Persius, were believed to have cut through falsehood and subterfuge to reveal facts about society that were unobscured by poetic invention or ornamentation.[16] Hence, a representative twelfth-century commentator on Juvenal can declare that 'satire is naked [...] because it censures the vices of the

---

[16] On the medieval literary theory of satire see especially Minnis and Scott, *Medieval Literary Theory*, pp. 116-18; Paul. S. Miller, 'The Mediaeval Literary Theory of Satire and its Relevance to the Works of Gower, Langland and Chaucer' (unpublished doctoral thesis, The Queen's University of Belfast, 1982), also his article 'John Gower, Satiric Poet', in *Gower's 'Confessio Amantis': Responses and Reassessments*, ed. by A.J. Minnis (Cambridge, 1983), pp. 79-105; U. Kindermann, *Satyra: Die Theorie der Satire im Mittellateinischen: Vorstudie zu einer Gattungsgeschichte* (Nuremberg, 1978).

Romans nakedly, and openly, and clearly, and without circumlocution and periphrasis, and without an *integumentum*'.[17] And Conrad of Hirsau, in comparing satyrs with satiric poets, explains that while the former are not embarrassed to expose themselves publicly without care for clothing (*nichil tractantes de tegumentis*), the latter are not restrained from their objective of making 'the depraved suffer under the naked outspokenness of their words'.[18] That is to say, it is unnecessary to interpret Roman satire allegorically because it conveys its moral message 'at the first, literal level of meaning', as Paul Miller puts it.[19] Obscure and obscuring *integumenta* were not deemed to be part and parcel of the style characteristic of satirists; here were no veils for the commentators to remove. For these authors spoke plainly and bluntly, getting straight to the point, even to the extent of being quite rude on occasion. Hence the satirists' language is often described as *fetidus*, *turpis*, even *obscenus*.[20] The outspokenness of Jean's Raison, her wish to call a spade a bloody shovel (or, to be more exact, to call testicles 'balls'), seems to be following in this tradition, and could well be a conscious development of it.

The full flavour of the *accessus ad satiricos* may be conveyed by one representative example, this being the introduction to Juvenal glosses which have been attributed to William of Conches by their modern editor, though this has proved controversial.[21] The vices of the Romans are identified as Juvenal's subject-matter (*materia*), and his mode of treatment (*modus agendi*) is reprehension (*reprehensio*), while the text's usefulness (*utilitas*) consists in the fact that it draws the reader or hearer (*auditor*) from the clutches of those vices. Our anonymous glossator proceeds to define satire in general as 'reprehension composed in metre' and then offers a possible explanation of the name: 'According to some, "satire" is so called from the satyrs, who were woodland gods, because the two are

---

[17] Cited from Oxford, Bodleian Library, MS Auct. F.6.9 by Miller, 'Literary Theory of Satire', p. 27; cf. Minnis and Scott, *Medieval Literary Theory*, p. 116.
[18] Minnis and Scott, *Medieval Literary Theory*, p. 61.
[19] Miller, 'Literary Theory of Satire', p. 27.
[20] See the quotations assembled by Miller, 'Literary Theory of Satire', p. 382, note 70.
[21] *Guillaume de Conches: Glosae in Iuvenalem*, ed. by Bradford Wilson, Textes philosophiques du moyen âge, 18 (Paris, 1980).

perfectly matched in all their characteristics', which include being naked and having 'an unbridled tongue'.

> They are naked and it is naked. For there are some writers who cover up (*velant*) their reprehension, as when Lucan, speaking of Nero's obesity, says: 'the axle will feel the weight' and then '[Nero will gaze on] Rome with oblique ray'. True satire consists of naked and open reprehension. Satyrs have an unbridled tongue; satire passes over no person in silence, and spares no one.[22]

Other *accessus* explain that the satirist was motivated by righteous anger (*indignatio*) or some similarly commendable reaction which led to an abrupt outburst (*ex abrupto*) against the ills of society.[23] While sparing no-one from his censure, he was careful to avoid spreading slander about particular individuals, and was fully prepared to admit his own failings.[24] Moreover, satire features a 'low' and 'light' (*levis*) rather than an elevated style: 'satira est levis quia constat vulgaribus verbis et cotidianis'.[25]

That remark, incidentally, points to the great potential of satiric writing *in vulgari*. One could be more vulgar in the vernacular, so

---

[22] Trans. from the Wilson edition, pp. 89-91, by Minnis and Scott, *Medieval Literary Theory*, pp. 134-38.

[23] For example, the Persius commentary attributed to Remigius of Auxerre speaks of the indignation, shock and urge to reprehend which motivated the satirist's outburst at the beginning of his first satire: 'Reprehendo cum indignatione et admiratione inchoavit et ipse ex abrupto, i. ex aspero docens [...]'. Cited by Dorothy M. Robathan and F. Edward Cranz (with P.O. Kristeller and B. Bischoff), 'A. Persius Flaccus', in *Catalogus translationum et commentariorum*, III, ed. by F. Edward Cranz and P.O. Kristeller (Washington, 1976), pp. 201-312 (p. 238). For similar statements see pp. 216, 219, 221. Cf. Miller, 'Literary Theory of Satire', pp. 101-03, 112.

[24] 'The satirists are in the habit of censuring even themselves', declares the *Scholia Pseudoacronis* on Horace; cited by Miller, 'John Gower, Satiric Poet', p. 93, who provides other examples of this view (see further p. 95).

[25] Robert John Barnett Jr., 'An Anonymous Medieval Commentary on Juvenal' (unpublished doctoral dissertation, University of N. Carolina at Chapel Hill, 1964), p. 1. Barnett dates this commentary to either the end of the twelfth century or early in the thirteenth; his edition is based on two manuscripts in the Bern Bürgerbibliothek, MSS 666 and A61. Similarly, in an *accessus* to a Juvenal commentary which represents the second of the vulgate traditions, a distinction is made between satire which, as it were, lives in the country and hence uses common words ('vulgaribus utitur verbis') and tragedy, which always uses elevated words ('regalibus utitur verbis'). Cited by Miller, 'John Gower, Satiric Poet', p. 97.

to speak, a fact which was fully appreciated by Walter of Châtillon (*c*.1135-after 1189), who composed several highly effective macaronic satires.[26]

Continuing with our review of the terms of reference of the *accessus ad satiricos*, it may be noted that irony is often identified as a feature of satire, and mockery and laughter are said to function to confute the vices: 'Deridendo etiam omnia redarguit vitia'.[27] Indeed, irony may be identified as satire's characteristic form of mockery: 'derisoria est, quod ironice loquitur'.[28]

Satiric discourse such as this—what Miller has called the 'vocabulary of censure'—is vitally important for an understanding both of Jean de Meun's *apologia* and for the style and strategy of his entire part of the *Rose*.[29] In order to acquire the relevant discourse Jean did not have to know the Roman satirists directly (though he certainly had read some Juvenal, on which more later), for the schoolroom *scholia* on those authors had helped to create a medieval satirical tradition, which flourished in the twelfth century, comprising texts by Walter of Châtillon and Walter Map and the *De contemptu mundi* of Bernard of Cluny (who died *c*.1140); an obvious later example is afforded by John of Garland's *Morale Scolarium* (1241), which was also known as the *Opus satiricum* or *Liber satiricum*. But wherever Jean got the relevant theoretical ideas from, they certainly are manifest in his *Rose*.

'Satire is the naked censure of vices, sparing no-one', declares a twelfth-century gloss on Juvenal.[30] And Walter of Châtillon's macaronic satire which begins 'A la feste sui venue' describes the

---

[26] Cf. Miller, 'John Gower, Satiric Poet', p. 86: 'Many poets found that the "low" style and abrasive tone of satire were more readily achieved in the vernacular languages than in the Latin of the Middle Ages from which vituperative colloquialisms had been refined'.
[27] Barnett, 'Anonymous Medieval Commentary on Juvenal', p. 2.
[28] Quoted from a thirteenth-century Persius gloss (in Bern, Bürgerbibliothek, MS 539b) by Miller, 'Literary Theory of Satire', p. 382, note 71.
[29] Miller, 'Literary Theory of Satire', p. 94.
[30] MS Auct. F.6.9, fol. 1r, cited by Miller, 'John Gower, Satiric Poet', p. 84. Cf. the 'William of Conches' Juvenal commentary: 'True satire consists of naked and open reprehension. Satyrs have an unbridled tongue; satire passes over no person in silence, and spares no one'. Trans. in Minnis and Scott, *Medieval Literary Theory*, p. 137.

poet-satirist as being 'like a sword sparing no guilty man'.[31] Similarly, Jean de Meun's self-construction professes himself to be no respecter of status or of persons (15221-26). Rather he seeks to wound hypocrites wherever they may be, whether they live in the world or in the cloister. It does not matter how they are clothed ('que robe qu'il se queuvre'), i.e. what office or role in society they perform—perhaps Jean was thinking here of satire's concern with the naked truth. *Nichil tractantes de tegumentis*.... However, it was not his *antancion*, Jean declares, to speak against any living man who follows holy religion or performs good works. He does not wish to harm anyone other than those who deserve his censure (15223-24; cf. 15231-45). Instead of having any specific target he shoots his arrows in a general fashion ('generaument'; 15227-30), using a volley—rather, one may presume, than aiming single shots at specific targets (cf. l.15245). Moreover, it is possible that the lines in which he declares that he does not wish to attack any 'fame qui soit en vie [...]' (15174-78) should be interpreted in a similar way, as meaning that the poet never said anything, nor intended to say anything, against any living woman in particular.

All this is reminiscent of the satirists' professed desire to avoid slandering individuals, their targets being people in general and indeed the vices in general. 'Vices are the subject-matter of the satirists, not the vices of a certain definite person considered individually (*non singulariter alicuius determinatae personae*), but rather those of the populace considered collectively (*populi communiter*)'.[32] And the opening lines of the *Morale Scolarium*[33] profess John of Garland's intention not to lacerate anyone in particular but rather to employ a style which will 'play' in general,

---

[31] *Moralisch-Satirische Gedichte Walters von Châtillon*, ed. by Karl Strecker (Heidelberg, 1929), p. 123 (no. 13); cited by Miller, 'John Gower, Satiric Poet', p. 84.

[32] From a twelfth-century Juvenal commentary found in Cologne, Dombibliothek MS 199; cited by E.M. Sanford, 'Juvenalis, Decimus Junius' in *Catalogus translationum et commentariorum*, I, ed. by F.E. Cranz and P.O. Kristeller (Washington, 1960), pp. 175-238 (p. 198). Cf. Miller, 'John Gower, Satiric Poet', p. 85.

[33] Ed. and trans. by Louis Paetow, Memoirs of the University of California, 4, no. 2 (Berkeley, 1927), pp. 65-273.

this presumably intimating the 'light' ('satira est levis') quality of satiric writing and its use of mockery:

> I am writing a new satire, but in order not to spread anger which is maddening, terrible, deadly and wounding, no one in particular will be slandered by the sharp words of a wicked man, but rather in such a style my pen will amuse itself in general terms.

Jean de Meun's phrasing and choice of expression are very much within this universe of discourse. Similar ideas, it may be added, are part and parcel of standard late-medieval theory of preaching.[34] In the eyes of some of their Christian readers, the Roman satirists seemed to anticipate the didactic techniques and appropriate lifestyles of the preachers of their own day. Indeed, sometimes the satirists were regarded as the preachers of antiquity.[35]

Finally, far from adopting a 'holier than thou' attitude, the first-person speaker of Jean's *apologia* frankly admits that he himself is a sinner ('quex que pechierres que je soie', 15228). Similarly, the Carolingian *Scholia Pseudoacronis* on Horace had declared that self-censure was commonly practised by the satirists,[36] a sentiment often echoed in later commentaries. For example, 'William of Conches' follows the 'Vulgate Scholia' by interpreting the opening lines of Juvenal's first satire as the poet's accusation of himself for having stayed silent for so long, this being done so that he could reprehend others the more freely: 'ut liberius consortes suos reprehendat,

---

[34] For a brief discussion, and references, see A.J. Minnis, 'Chaucer's Pardoner and the "Office of Preacher"', in *Intellectuals and Writers in Fourteenth-Century Europe*, ed. by P. Boitani and A. Torti, Tübinger Beiträge zur Anglistik, 7 (Tübingen and Cambridge, 1986), pp. 88-119 (pp. 107-08).
[35] As Miller says, they 'illustrated and censured the moral shortcomings of their pagan society in words that would endear them to many a Christian apologist. Like the preachers of the Christian Middle Ages, the Roman satirists recognised the spiritual deficiencies of their world and, through admonition, attempted to rectify its moral shortcomings' ('Literary Theory of Satire', pp. 26-27). See further Bernard Bischoff's account of a Juvenal commentary (*Catalogus* I, 196ff.) in which Christian equivalents are found for the rites and tenets of pagan religion: 'Living with the Satirists', in *Classical Influences on European Culture, A.D. 500-1500*, ed. by R.R. Bolgar (Cambridge, 1971), pp. 83-94 (pp. 89-90).
[36] See note 24 above.

seipsum in principio de nimia taciturnitate reprehendit'.[37] In another version of this same gloss, the rhetorical question is asked, 'How can a man who does not spare himself spare either you or me?'[38] By refusing to spare himself, therefore, Jean de Meun is justifying his refusal to spare others.

Given the evidence here reviewed, it is little wonder that that great defender of Jean de Meun in the *querelle de la Rose*, Jean de Montreuil, should describe him as a 'very severe satirist' (*satiricum perseverum*).[39] This is, of course, meant as a great compliment, as is made utterly clear by the fact that it is accompanied by the affirmation that truth will conquer, while false things do not last. It may be concluded, therefore, that knowledge of medieval notions about the naked text of satire played a significant role in Jean de Meun's self-fashioning as a poet.

Ovid among the satirists

Jean's indebtedness to satiric theory, as understood in his day, was not limited to the *apologia*, but may be said to have touched his text at many significant points. Raison is not the only figure in the *Rose* who speaks with a directness which is blunt to the point of rudeness. Moreover, Jean demonstrates direct knowledge of passages from the Roman satirists themselves, his love of Juvenal being particularly obvious. For example, at ll. 8251ff., when Ami is complaining about how women are not satisfied until they have got everything they possibly can out of their lovers, he follows the general statement of 'Juvenaus', 'Never will you find a woman who spares the man who

---

[37] From the text represented in Paris, Bibliothèque Nationale, MS Lat. 2904; *Glosae in Iuvenalem*, ed. Wilson, p. 92.
[38] Found in Baltimore, Walters Art Gallery, MS 20; *Glosae in Iuvenalem*, ed. Wilson, p. 92.
[39] Letter *Etsi facundissimus*, in *Le Débat sur le 'Roman de la Rose'*, ed. by Eric Hicks (Paris, 1977), p. 38; cf. the translation by Joseph L. Baird and John R. Kane, *La Querelle de la Rose: Letters and Documents*, North Carolina Studies in the Romance Languages and Literatures, 199 (Chapel Hill, 1978), p. 44. Similarly, in his letter *Ut sunt mores*, Jean complains that the *Rose*'s detractors 'simply do not understand how that teacher [i.e. de Meun] has fulfilled the function of a satirist (*satirici is instructor fungitur officio*) and is therefore permitted many things which are prohibited to other writers', which I assume means that the satirist is allowed a certain stylistic license which is denied to those who produce other kinds of writing (ed. Hicks, p. 42; trans. Baird and Kane, p. 154).

loves her; for though she be herself aflame, she delights to torment and plunder him' (*Satura* VI, 208-10).⁴⁰ This is conflated with Juvenal's specific attack on Hibernia, who is not satisfied with one man any more than she would be satisfied with one eye (*Satura* VI, 53-54), here misunderstood (or should one say reworked?) to mean, 'she would rather lose one of her eyes than be attached to one man' (8259-60). Jean then moves on to praise the Golden Age (8325ff.) in which women had other customs: loves were loyal and pure then, without greed or rapine (8329-30). This echoes the opening lines of Juvenal's sixth satire, in which the poet looks back to the 'days of Saturn' in which 'Chastity still lingered on the earth' (1-2).

Given that this is the Roman poet's most thoroughgoing piece of antifeminist writing, it is quite understandable that Jean should move on to have Ami present the figure of the Jealous Husband as commending Theophrastus's 'Golden Book' on marriage (8531ff.), known only through Jerome's citations in that other classic of misogyny, the *Adversus Jovinianum*. And in turn this is followed by Walter Map's *Dissuasio Valerii ad Ruffinum philosophum ne uxorem ducat* (8575ff.).⁴¹ Jean de Meun may well have read Map's epistle as a satire. For it begins *ex abrupto*, in the best satirical manner: 'I am forbidden to speak, and I cannot keep silence'.⁴² That phrasing recalls Juvenal's first satire, commonly interpreted by the glossators as the Roman poet's profession of his compulsion to write (in view of the vices of his contemporaries, which cried out for censure) despite the pressures on him to keep silent.⁴³ 'I hate the

---

⁴⁰ I have used the edition and translation by G.G. Ramsay, *Juvenal and Persius* (Cambridge, Mass., and London, rev. edn 1940).
⁴¹ Jean actually draws on 'Valerius' before his ostentatious naming of him at ll. 8659, 8689 and 8697; ll. 8575-78 and 8621-22 follow the *Dissuasio*, expanding it with the story of Lucrece as told by Livy (cf. Lecoy's note on p. 273). Juvenal himself is named again at l. 8705: here Jean is following *Satura* VI. 28-32; he seems also to have used Juvenal at ll. 8674-86 (cf. *Sat.* VI. 165, 47-49) and maybe at l. 8665 (cf. Sat. VII. 202).
⁴² Walter Map, *De Nugis curialium. Courtiers' Trifles*, ed. and trans. by M.R. James, revised by C.N.L. Brooke and R.A.B. Mynors (Oxford, 1983), pp. 288-89.
⁴³ See for example the two versions of the relevant 'William of Conches' gloss as edited by Wilson, *Glosae in Iuvenalem*, p. 92. The Paris manuscript reads: 'Sed ut liberius consortes suos reprehendat, seipsum in principio de minia taciturnitate reprehendit'. Thus in the usual satiric manner Juvenal begins with an exclamation which is prompted by indignation: 'ita more satirico ex indignatione clamando

crane and the screech-owl's voice', Map continues; 'I hate the owl and the other birds that dismally shriek their prophecies of the woes of winter and mud'.[44] That is to say, he has no wish to act like those proverbial prophets of doom. Yet speak out he must—and, of course, he does.

This combination of materials, therefore, has its own logic. What may seem less comprehensible is why Ami should wish to follow those particular authorities in the first place. Given that his ostensible mission in the poem is to help the lover into his desired rose-bed, why should so many of Ami's remarks be of a type which could well put the lover off women altogether? The basic answer is that in the *Rose* the agendas of satire and of seduction seem remarkably intertwined on occasion. We may focus our attention on the problem by noting that, shortly before the specific citations of Juvenal's sixth satire as discussed above, Ami had offered over 500 lines of advice, culled from Ovid's *Ars amatoria*, on the best methods of courtship (*Rose*, 7277ff.). These involve making strong promises, swearing vehement oaths, weeping profusely (with some tips on how to fake it, if need be), and winning over the lady's guardians with gifts, flattery, or any other means necessary. In short, this is a training in the art of deception, as Amant himself points out (though subsequently, of course, he will do what his friend suggested). It leads naturally enough into a derogatory account of the ways of women.

---

incipit'. Cf. the typical glosses on Persius's opening exclamation, as cited in note 23 above.

[44] Aesculapius was changed into a screech-owl for reporting that Proserpine had violated Pluto's law by eating three apple seeds: an *exemplum* of being forbidden to speak yet being unable to keep silent. Perhaps Map had this *fabula* in mind. It appears in Ovid, *Metamorphoses*, 5, 539-52, where the screech owl is described as a bird 'which heralds impending disaster, a harbinger of woe for mortals' (trans. by Mary M. Innes (Harmondsworth, 1955), p. 130). On the owl as a prophet of doom see further Alan of Lille, *De planctu naturae*, II, pr.1 (trans. by J.J. Sheridan (Toronto, 1980), pp. 89-90), and the Early Middle English poem (perhaps of the twelfth century) *The Owl and the Nightingale*, ll. 329ff., 925, 1261-68; ed. E.G. Stanley (Manchester and New York, rev. edn 1970), pp. 59-60, 76, 85. The crane was commonly regarded as a bird with a strong, complaining cry; the leader of a flock of cranes would force the others to fly away, 'crienge as hit were blamynge' with her voice: *On the Properties of Things. John Trevisa's Translation of Bartholomaeus Anglicus, 'De Proprietatibus rerum'*, ed. by M.C. Seymour *et al.* (Oxford, 1975), p. 626.

Here we are in the world of *Ovidius minor*, a very different writer from the revered *auctor* of that 'pagan Bible', the *Metamorphoses*, a work which was highly susceptible to Christian appropriation and moralization. Ovid's love-poetry was composed to entertain a sophisticated audience of young aristocrats, who would find in the *Ars amatoria* at once sexual comedy, seduction techniques, and worldly cynicism—an unstable mixture of the serious and the scurrilous, the elevated and the obscene, which (so to speak) became even more volatile in the hands of its medieval readers. This may briefly be illustrated by the preface to *L'Art d'amours*, a translation into French of the *Ars amatoria* along with traditional gloss materials, the first part of which was produced sometime between 1214 and 1233.[45] The approach taken follows in the footsteps of the Latin *accessus* to the *Ars*, one of the reasons which moved Ovid to write being identified as his wish 'to teach his friends and companions the art of love, or to teach them how to win the love of women and young girls'.[46] 'There are some young men who love young women very much', the anonymous translator continues, 'but they do not know how to court them, or how to find them, or how to do the things that would win them'. So they may despair, and either kill themselves or go mad. It was 'in order to remove this despair from the hearts of the young' that Ovid wrote this book. But our writer is not content to leave the matter there. Another reason why Ovid wrote was 'to reveal the fickleness of his youth'.[47] The poet, 'when he was an adolescent and when he was a

---

[45] This work has been edited by Bruno Roy, *L'Art d'amours. Traduction et commentaire de l'Ars amatoria d'Ovide* (Leiden, 1974) and translated by Lawrence B. Blonquist, *L'Art d'amours (The Art of Love)*, Garland Library of Medieval Literature, Series A, 32 (New York and London, 1987). Blonquist's introduction is marred by minor errors, which may be typographical, though it is disconcerting to find the plural of *accessus* being given as *accessi* on three occasions. A fuller account of *L'Art d'amours* is given in my own forthcoming article, 'Latin to Vernacular: Academic Prologues and the Medieval French Art of Love'.

[46] *L'Art d'amours*, ed. Roy, p. 63; trans. Blonquist, p. 1. Cf. for example the *accessus* to the *Ars amatoria* trans. in Minnis and Scott, *Medieval Literary Theory*, p. 24: 'His purpose in this work is to instruct young men in the art of love, and how they should behave towards girls when having a love-affair. [...] The way he proceeds in this work is to show how a girl may be picked up (*possit inveniri*), how when picked up she may be won over, and, once won over, how her love may be retained'.

[47] *L'Art d'amours*, ed. Roy, p. 63; trans. Blonquist, p. 1.

young man, wrote this book in the first flower of his age and of his life'.[48] This puts the *Ars amatoria* firmly in its place, both physiologically and morally. When this anonymous translation was produced, the notion that youth was the age in which men were particularly susceptible to love, given that this was the time at which their bodily heat was at its greatest, was an utter commonplace, along with the concomitant that in one's maturity wiser counsels would, or at least should, prevail.[49] Elsewhere in medieval scholarship on Ovid an historical location and placing of the *Ars* takes place, as when this work of his youth is said to have been condemned by the Emperor Augustus and others, who judged it to be immoral; Ovid wrote the *Remedium amoris* in an attempt to retract the doctrine of his earlier poem, but to no avail, for he was forced into exile.[50]

The implications of these facts of medieval literary scholarship for interpretation of the *Rose* are many and various. What is most obvious, I hope, is that a structure which is built on so unstable a foundation as the *Ovidius minor* is itself likely to be highly unstable, offering materials which are capable of being taken in many different ways. Given that Jean de Meun greatly amplified all of the contesting Ovidian elements, it may be suggested (certainly, it is what I believe) that he magnified that instability rather than bringing it under control.

Two more specific points may be ventured here. First, given the ambivalent nature of the *Ars* itself (a courtship manual which nevertheless reveals the follies of youth), along with the fact that in

---

[48] *L'Art d'amours*, ed. Roy, p. 69; trans. Blonquist, p. 4. For Ovid as a poet who wrote love-poetry in his youth and/or who addressed a youthful audience see the relevant remarks in the *accessus* printed by Minnis and Scott, *Medieval Literary Theory*, pp. 24, 25, 27, 362; F. Ghisalberti, 'Mediaeval Biographies of Ovid', *Journal of the Warburg and Courtauld Institutes*, 9 (1946), 10-59 (pp. 44, 45, 47, 51, 57, 59); Ralph J. Hexter, *Ovid and Medieval Schooling. Studies in Medieval School Commentaries on Ovid's 'Ars Amatoria', 'Epistulae ex Ponto', and 'Epistulae Heroidum'* (Munich, 1986), p. 219.
[49] See J.A. Burrow, *The Ages of Man. A Study in Medieval Writing and Thought* (Oxford, 1986), p. 157.
[50] See for example the *vita Ovidii* of Arnulf of Orléans, in Ghisalberti, 'Arnolfo d'Orléans', pp. 180-81, repr. by A.G. Elliott, '*Accessus ad auctores*: Twelfth-Century Introductions to Ovid', *Allegorica*, 5.1 (1980), 6-48 (pp. 12-17). And also the *accessus* to the *Remedium amoris* translated by Minnis and Scott, *Medieval Literary Theory*, p. 25.

medieval scholarship the *Ars* and the *Remedium amoris* went together like the proverbial horse and carriage, Ovid being regarded as the expert on both the pursuit and the eradication of love, material from his shorter poems could be taken as emitting either positive or negative signals about human desire—or indeed, confused signals, which could be decoded either way. Given this pliancy of *Ovidius minor*, it is hardly surprising to find him, in Ami's monologue, rubbing shoulders with Juvenal, Jerome and Walter Map. They are definitely in agreement about the deficiencies of womankind—and the question of whether those deficiences are to be condemned or exploited is less important than that large measure of agreement. Theorists sometimes distinguished between Ovid and the satirists on the grounds that the intention of the former was solely to delight, and of the latter, to teach;[51] practising poets, however, often recognised that they had spoken with one voice.[52] Hence the conflation of Ovid and Juvenal, as noted above, with perhaps some help from the *Dissuasio Valerii*, particularly if Jean de Meun had recognised its formal affinities with the genre of satire. Ovid has become, it could be said, an honorary satirist.

The occasional consonance (from Jean's point of view) of these poets' style and substance may be illustrated further by Jean's citation of *Satura* I, 38-39 at *Rose* 21409-412: 'Juvenal declares that if a man wants to gain a great fortune he can take no shorter road than to take up with a rich old woman'. This, as the context of this declaration in Juvenal's text makes clear, is one of the many things which today's guilty age presents to his gaze in the open street (cf. ll. 63-64), arousing his indignation and obliging him to write 'angry

---

[51] See the discussion by A.J. Minnis, 'Theorizing the Rose: Commentary Tradition in the *Querelle de la Rose*', in *Poetics: Theory and Practice in Medieval English Literature*, ed. by P. Boitani and A. Torti (Cambridge, 1991), pp. 13-36 (pp. 23-25).

[52] Moreover, this was certainly the view of Jean Gerson, a fierce critic of Jean de Meun in the *querelle de la Rose*, who lumped together Juvenal and Ovid, along with other sources of the *Rose*, in this thoroughgoing condemnation: 'this romance contains not only Ovid's *Art of Loving*, but also other books which are there translated, brought together, and drawn in by force and to no purpose. Meun used both Ovid and the works of others, which are not any the less dishonourable or dangerous, like the writings of Heloise and Abelard, and of Juvenal [...]'. See *Le Débat*, ed. Hicks, pp. 76-77; trans. Baird and Kane, p. 83.

rhymes'.[53] But Jean de Meun connects it to Ovid's recommendation of women of 'a later age' (*Ars amatoria*, ii.667-68).[54] Ovid was making the point that older women make better lovers; Jean de Meun, however, follows Juvenal's lead in emphasising the financial rather than the sexual rewards. Then he declares that older women are harder to trap because they have passed the time of their youth, when they were very susceptible to flattery and liable to be taken in and tricked; the implicit conclusion is that it is better for a man to try his luck with young women, who are less wary of the traps— women, it may be inferred, like the virgin Rose herself. Here it is difficult if not impossible to decide if Ovid has once again been made (or allowed) to speak like a satirist or if, thanks to Jean's (or is it Amant's?) casuistry, Juvenal has been enlisted in the ranks of the *praeceptores amoris*.

Whichever discourse (the erotic or the satiric) one judges to be dominant in such passages, it seems abundantly clear that it is not integumental, the meaning being very much on the surface, made manifest in an aggressively direct and frank manner; there does not seem to be any wish to bury significance deep under the surface where it can be reached only by the expert probing of *cognoscenti*. And that is my second specific point regarding Jean de Meun's exploitation of materials from the *Ovidius minor*, and of the various resonances which they struck in the minds of medieval scholiasts.

I would suggest further that, to a considerable extent, in Jean's poem the mythographic language of the *Ovidius maior*, with all its potential for allegoresis, has been assimilated to the *modus loquendi* characteristic of the *Ovidius minor*. This argument may be advanced through an investigation of his exploitations of several *fabulae poetarum* which owed much of their medieval reputation to their inclusion in the *Metamorphoses*.[55]

---

[53] Here I draw on the translation by William Gifford, *Juvenal, Satires, with the Satires of Persius* (London, 1992), pp. 6, 11.
[54] I have used Ovid, *'The Art of Love' and Other Poems*, ed. by J.H. Mozley (London and Cambridge, Mass., 1939).
[55] Limitations of space preclude a full discussion of Jean's handling of mythographic materials, but the examples I have chosen are, in my view, quite representative of his practice throughout the *Rose*.

Ovid unveiled

The fable of Venus and Adonis (as recorded in *Metamorphoses* X) is referred to by way of introduction to Venus, when Jean's narrative reaches the point at which that deity's aid is sought by the Castle's attackers. In his *Metamorphoses* commentary Arnulf of Orléans, following and elaborating upon Fulgentius, had declared that the death of Adonis signifies the extinction of love's pleasure, whether it be in the work of Venus or in any other activity; his transformation into a flower is taken as an affirmation of the superiority of charitable love over the love of Venus.[56] In the *Rose*, however, the 'moral' which is drawn (as part and parcel of Jean's erotic *comoedia*) is that lovers should believe their sweethearts; moreover, he pokes fun at the protagonists by depicting Venus as a scold and Adonis as a childish character who turns a deaf ear to her constant nagging (cf. 15645ff.).

A similar process is at work in Jean's appropriation of the fable of Hercules and Cacus, as alluded to in *Metamorphoses* IX and treated more fully in Boethius, *De consolatione philosophiae*, iv. met.vii. Fulgentius had explained that 'Cacus' is from the Greek word *cacon*, which means 'evil'.[57] He 'covets the property of Hercules, because all evil is opposed to virtue', and hides Hercules' cattle 'in his cave because evil is never frank or open-faced; but virtue slays the evil ones and redeems its own possessions'. Thieves like Cacus create smoke in an attempt to conceal their wrongdoing; thus evil 'puts out either what is contrary to the truth, that is, light, or what is offensive to those who see it, as smoke is to the eyes, or what is dark and dismal raillery. And so evil in its manifold forms is two-faced, not straightforward [...]'. In the thirteenth-century revision of William of Conches's Boethius commentary,[58] the episode

---

[56] Ghisalberti, 'Arnolfo d'Orléans', p. 223. Cf. Fulgentius's account of the fable of Myrrha and Adonis, *Mitologiarum libri tres*, iii.8; trans. by Leslie George Whitbread, *Fulgentius the Mythographer* (Columbus, Ohio, 1971), p. 92.

[57] *Mit.*, ii.3; trans. Whitbread, pp. 68-69.

[58] Jean de Meun seems to have known a version of this thirteenth-century commentary, and used it both in the *Rose* and in his translation of *De consolatione philosophiae*: see A.J. Minnis, 'Aspects of the Medieval French and English Traditions of the *De consolatione philosophiae*', in *Boethius. His Life, Thought and Influence*, ed. by M.T. Gibson (Oxford, 1981), pp. 312-61 (pp. 315-34). For proof that this commentary is not the work of William of Conches himself see A.J.

of Hercules and Cacus is interpreted in terms of how evil seeks to lead right reason astray and wishes to hide under malice, but Hercules, i.e. the wise man, extracts, kills and despoils Cacus (literally 'strips him', *denudatur*), thus bringing hidden malice out into the open.[59] Similarly, William of Aragon talks of how the *sapiens* diligently shuns evil in all things, avoiding it himself and also teaching its avoidance to others;[60] once again, the actual extraction and killing of Cacus is interpreted as all that is sordid and invidious being brought into the open.[61] All this is a far cry from ll. 15526-62 of the *Rose*, where Seürtez ('Security'), in criticising Poor ('Fear'), recalls how Poor fled with Cacus when he saw Hercules come running towards him with his club. And from ll. 21589-602, when Amant's difficult penetration of his virgin rose is likened to the force which Hercules has to use to break into the cave of Cacus. The first passage offers exemplary narrative, which needs to be read *litteraliter*; the second, a very literal joke. In both these cases, as in the Ovidian narrative of Venus and Adonis, Jean's text seems to have divested *fabulae* of the integuments in which moralising clerics had clothed them.

When the *Rose* does indeed appear to be drawing on traditions of moralising mythography, the effect is often quite different from that found in the earlier texts. Jean de Meun, and indeed Guillaume de Lorris before him, were not content to reflect those traditions passively, but rather made vital contributions to them. Excellent examples are afforded by the uses to which the *fabulae* of Narcissus and Pygmalion (cf. *Metamorphoses* III and X respectively) are put in the poem. There is a remarkable degree of consensus among its modern readers regarding the status of the fountain of Narcissus as

---

Minnis and Lodi Nauta, '*More Platonico loquitur*: What Nicholas Trevet really did to William of Conches', in *Chaucer's 'Boece'*, ed. Minnis, pp. 1-33. See further Lodi Nauta's appendix, on pp. 189-91.

[59] London, British Library, MS Royal 15.B.III, fol. 122r. A similar account is given in William's own commentary, but it should be noted that in the copy of it which I consulted, Troyes, Bibliothèque Municipale, MS 1381, fol. 84r, the verb 'diuiditur' is used instead of the Royal MS's 'denudatur'.

[60] For Jean de Meun's knowledge of at least the prologue to the Boethius commentary of William of Aragon (who flourished in the second half of the thirteenth century) see Minnis, 'Medieval French and English Traditions', pp. 314, 315-34.

[61] Paris, Bibliothèque Nationale, MS Lat. 11,856, fol. 111r.

'an emblem of destructive self-love',[62] though it must be said that this interpretation is hardly in the mainstream of integumental analysis of that Ovidian fable. For Arnulf of Orléans, for instance, Narcissus can be understood as arrogance, while Echo means a man's good fame. She speaks well of arrogance, who however rejects her and prefers himself. For this he is turned into a flower, i.e. a useless thing, because he quickly passes away in the manner of a flower.[63] In short, Guillaume de Lorris pays more attention to the fable's *sensus litteralis* than Arnulf does, the theme of self-love being utterly apparent if the Ovidian text is read as exemplary narrative.

Even more remarkably, Jean de Meun sets up Pygmalion as the antithesis of Narcissus, this being part and parcel of a systematic recapitulation and redirection of Guillaume's major terms of reference which begins around 1.20339. Initially at least, Pygmalion is no less a fool than Narcissus, despite his foolish protestation that his situation is different, since Narcissus could not possess what he saw in the fountain whereas he, Pygmalion, can take, embrace and kiss his beloved ivory statue (20843-58). But this is, of course, no genuine possession, as Pygmalion himself admits a few lines later: 'I find my love as rigid as a post and so very cold that my mouth is chilled when I touch her to kiss her' (20871-76). It would have been the easiest thing in the world for Jean to have depicted Pygmalion as an emblem of perverted desire—a figure just like Narcissus. After all, Arnulf of Orléans had stated that 'In truth, Pygmalion the wonderful artificer made an ivory statue which he began to misuse as though it were a living woman (*cepit abuti ad modum vere mulieris*)'.[64] However, Jean does not present Pygmalion as doing disgusting things with a sex toy. He follows not the gloss of Arnulf but the text of Ovid, wherein Venus answers Pygmalion's prayers and turns the statue into a living woman, who bears him a child,

---

[62] As Thomas D. Hill puts it; 'Narcissus, Pygmalion, and the Castration of Saturn: Two Mythographical Themes in the *Roman de la Rose*', *Studies in Philology*, 71 (1974), pp. 404-26 (p. 407). Cf. Wetherbee, 'Literal and Allegorical', pp. 268-69, 285-86.
[63] Ghisalberti, 'Arnolfo d'Orléans', p. 209.
[64] Ghisalberti, 'Arnolfo d'Orléans', p. 223.

Paphos, from which the island of Paphos takes its name.[65] In short, the farcical courtship of an inanimate object (which may well be taken as emblematic of the ridiculous adulation which some lovers profess in order to win their ladies) nevertheless results in the continuation of a man's divine self through progeny, to borrow a phrase from Raison (4373-80), and as such is a cut above the sterile self-love exemplified by the behaviour of Narcissus, which had no issue. Moreover, as regarded in these terms, Jean's version of the Pygmalion legend rightly precedes the consummation of Amant's love for his Rose, an encounter which may have resulted in her impregnation (depending on how one interprets ll. 21699-700) but which certainly involves 'natural' heterosexual practice of the type recommended by Alan de Lille.[66] However, Jean problematises rather than follows the prescriptive sexuality of *De planctu naturae* by intermingling the discourse of aggressive Ovidian eroticism, replete with its cross-currents of mysogyny and cynicism.

It could be argued, then, that in large measure Jean has lifted the veils from Ovidian *fabulae*, the possibilities for integumental allegoresis being spurned in favour of *exemplum*, and indeed of euhemerism, by which I mean a strategy of humanization.[67] However, integuments are indeed to be found in the *Rose*. And they come not from Raison (despite her mention of the *theory* of the interpretative method) or indeed from the narrator/Amant despite the suggestion that he may gloss the poet's sentences, fables and metaphors in time (7160-68). Others may defer, but the figure who delivers is—Genius.

---

[65] This point is emphasized by Hill, who argues that the tradition whereby Pygmalion 'is an emblem of sterile and perverted concupiscence, is simply not relevant to the *Roman de la Rose*' ('Narcissus, Pygmalion', pp. 409-10).
[66] On Alan's doctrine of sexuality see the discussion by Sheridan in the introduction to his translation of *De planctu naturae*, pp. 40-41, 59-62, and especially Joan Cadden, *Meanings of Sex Difference in the Middle Ages* (Cambridge, 1993), pp. 209, 221-25.
[67] For a cogent introduction to medieval euhemeristic techniques see John D. Cooke, 'Euhemerism: A Medieval Interpretation of Classical Paganism', *Speculum*, 2 (1927), 396-410.

Integumanz at last: The Garments of Genius

Of course, Genius's credentials as exegete have been viewed with intense suspicion. 'Genius, like Amis, La Vieille, and above all the Lover himself' is regarded as 'unregeneratedly carnal and literal' by John Fleming, who reads the 'comedy and ironic inadequacy' of his 'pontifical pronouncements' as part of a strategy which seeks to direct the text's readers towards moral condemnation of Nature's priest.[68] And yet: the 'sermon' of Genius contains the most substantial use of allegoresis in Jean's text, comprising not only *integumanz aus poetes* but theological symbolism as well. For it is Genius who, *inter alia*, describes the life of the blessed in Paradise, and affirms the superiority of the Good Shepherd's Park over the Garden of Mirth (as described at the beginning of the poem, by Guillaume), a critique which is of course central to the panallegorists' reading of the poem. Surely they should give Genius the credit for that, at least? Not that they do, of course.

True, on occasion Jean seems to want to remind us of who is actually speaking here. For instance, Genius recommends the *Rose* as a book which will ensure that its readers need not fear the judgment of Rhadamanthus, Aeacus and Minos, going on to claim that the leading of a good life involves loyalty in love, with each lover pleasing the other (19855-60). Later, he declares that those who teach Nature's doctrine will not be kept out of Paradise (19901ff.). The winning of heaven is indubitably a more complicated business than that! And Genius indulges his castration complex (20007-52), even making the absurd threat—a joke that has fallen flat for many modern readers—that mass castration should be inflicted on those who fail to follow Nature's laws. But the proposition that therefore everything he says should be regarded as suspect is simply too much to swallow. Indeed, even Fleming admits that some of his comments have some value: 'while Genius himself is totally amoral he knows (rather than understands) that the path of mythography leads very quickly to Christian morality, so he also knows that the likely consequence of following the dispensation of Jupiter is eternal damnation in a hell which is the negation of the

---

[68] Fleming, *Allegory and Iconography*, p. 210.

Good Shepherd's Paradise'.[69] Not bad for a 'buffoon' who knows nothing of grace, and whose appropriation of symbolic language is in Fleming's view 'unregeneratedly carnal and literal'![70]

The following brief review of Genius's sermon will, I hope, serve to demonstrate that this construct is better regarded as a site occupied by several, sometimes competing, discourses rather than as a figure who must always speak 'in character'; or, to put it a little differently, that in Jean's *Rose* discourses are not strictly constrained by the requirements of *persona*-definition.[71] Nature sends Genius out to preach that those who strive against her laws will be excommunicated while those who repent, and vigorously strive to multiply the human race, will receive a total pardon for all their sins against her. But what begins as an exhortation to Love's barons to practise natural sex (as opposed to the perversions which Alan of Lille had attacked) and thereby save their family lines from oblivion, moves into a forceful account of the three fatal sisters who bear, spin and cut the thread of life, along with Cerberus the hound of hell who longs to feed off men's flesh. This evocation of the terrors of the other world, wherein the denizens of the classical Hades are given qualities characteristic of those tormenting devils who inhabit the Christian Hell, goes far beyond what is necessary for the encouragement of Cupid's army.

It is as if the discourse relating to the underworld is following its own logic. Talk of the unavoidable pagan inferno prompts an affirmation of the infinitely preferable Christian equivalent, when the hope is expressed that God, who is Nature's master, may save the narrator when Atropos buries him; 'He is the salvation of body and soul [...]' (19867-69). Soon the text is elaborating the attractions of the Christian (Heavenly) Paradise, a land of beautiful fields wherein

---

[69] Fleming, *Allegory and Iconography*, p. 222.
[70] Fleming, *Allegory and Iconography*, p. 210, cf. p. 208.
[71] On medieval *persona*-theory see Minnis, 'Theorizing the Rose', pp. 14-22. The liberties which Jean de Meun sometimes takes with his *personae* were criticized by Jean Gerson, who complained about the 'corrupt' way in which Alan of Lille's character Nature was used in the *Rose*, and about how 'inappropriate opinions' were attributed to certain characters ('il atribue a la personne qui parle ce qui ne le doit appartenir'), 'as when he introduces Nature speaking of Paradise and the mysteries of our Faith [...]'. In *Le Débat*, ed. Hicks, pp. 80, 85; trans. Baird and Kane, pp. 86, 89.

the offspring of a virgin ewe leads His white sheep along a scarcely trodden, narrow path which is covered with flowers and herbs. There they can eat their fill, and no harm will befall them, thanks to the attentions of the Good Shepherd (19877ff.). After this excursus, the text returns to secular symbolism, in recuperating the myth of the Golden Age which came to an end with the castration of Saturn—a *narratio fabulosa* which, of course, was first introduced by Raison (20053ff.). The final verses of Genius's description of the Fall from that pagan Eden link with the previous narrative block, in distinguishing between two kinds of sheep, the black ones with meagre fleeces who never will be released by the infernal gods (described as having taken the broad path, which has led to the miserable dwelling they now occupy),[72] and the white, smooth and sleek ones who enjoy life in the Shepherd's Park (20179ff.). Genius then proceeds to offer a thoroughgoing critique of the Garden of Mirth (20305ff.), with special emphasis being placed on the 'perilous fountain, so bitter and poisonous' which killed Narcissus (20379-82). By the time he has finished no-one could possibly doubt that the Park's Fountain of Life is superior in every way. Then the narrative reasserts itself; Genius remembers who 'he' is. The text speaks once more of Nature's promise of Pardon and threat of excommunication within the sphere of sexuality, and Love's barons prepare for the final assault on the Castle of Jealousy (20653ff.).

The subsequent narrative is a far cry from, say, the symbolism of the carbuncle placed in the Fountain of Life, which is perfectly round (betokening eternity) and of three facets, an obvious image of the Trinity (20495-503). What Genius (of all people, so to speak) has given us is no less than a powerful vision—a *visio imaginaria*, to use the technical term—of the final judgment, with heaven and hell being presented in all their stark oppositions.[73] Moreover, it is perfectly possible to find in his words an affirmation of the superiority of heavenly love over all earthly love (though it is also

---

[72] In contrast with the narrow path taken by the abovementioned white sheep. Of course the image of the two roads derives from Matthew 7. 13-14.

[73] But imaginary vision was not the highest type of vision; that was the intellectual vision, which precluded imagery, though it could be argued that *visio imaginaria* included a certain amount of *visio intellectualis*. See A.J. Minnis, 'Langland's Ymaginatif and Late-Medieval Theories of Imagination', *Comparative Criticism*, 3 (1981), 71-103 (pp. 92-94).

possible to argue, in the light of what comes next in the poem, that sterile, unproductive earthly love is being specifically criticized by Jean). Whatever view one takes on that issue, it seems remarkable that Genius, whose domain is earthly love and generation, should have pronounced on matters which are far beyond his ken. Here is no figure who simply and exclusively lends 'spurious authority' to the 'devious plot' being hatched by those 'forces of carnal license who have installed him as a puppet bishop'.[74] For at least *some* of the things Genius says are redolent of real authority, possess genuine spiritual value. At any rate, many of Jean's early readers seem to have been quite unworried by the fact that his amalgam of paradisal imagery from scriptural and secular sources is attributed to Genius. For, as Fleming himself admits, certain illuminators were very interested in highlighting this eschatology.[75] It may be added that several fourteenth-century scribes 'could gloss the discourse of Genius as an allegory of Christian Heaven and salvation'[76] while Pierre Col, within the *querelle* of the *Rose*, could read Genius's criticism of the Garden of Delight as a direct statement of the views of the author, proof positive that Master Jean de Meun was not himself a foolish lover:

> Conment pouoit il mieux monstrer qu'il n'estoit pas fol amoureux et qu'il amoit Raison que en blasment le vergier Deduit et les choses qui y sont, et en louant Raison et mettant ung aultre parc (ung autre parc ou vergier), ouquel il figure si notablement la Trinitey et l'Incarnacion par l'escharboucle et par l'olive qui prant son acroissement de la rousee de la fontainne, etc.?

> [How could he show better that he was not a foolish lover and that he loved Reason than by blaming the Garden of Delight and the things that are in it; and by praising Reason and by presenting another park (another park or garden), in which he depicts so nobly the Trinity and the Incarnation by the

---

[74] Fleming, *Allegory and Iconography*, p. 211.
[75] Fleming, *Allegory and Iconography*, p. 222 (and Fig.7). See further Sylvia Huot, *The 'Roman de la Rose' and its Medieval Readers* (Cambridge, 1993), pp. 30-31. Her subsequent discussion brings out very well how the discourse of Genius 'had always been susceptible of divergent readings'.
[76] Huot, *Medieval Readers*, p. 175.

carbuncle and by the olive tree which takes its growth from the dew of the fountain, etc.]⁷⁷

Indeed, Col ends this particular document by echoing that very same disquisition of Jean's:

> [...] laquelle nous ottroit a tous toison si blanche que nous puissiens, avec le dit de Meung, brouter de herbes qui sont ou parc a l'aignelet saillant.

> [And may the Trinity grant us all a fleece so white that we may, with the said de Meun, crop the grass which grows in the park of the little gamboling lamb.]⁷⁸

And surely it was the sermon of Genius which must have moved Laurent de Premierfait to compare the *Rose* with Dante's *Comedy* as texts which treated of heaven and hell.⁷⁹

In short, to this *persona* is entrusted the allegorical centrepiece or climax of the entire text, an excursus which in its spirituality far transcends everything which has come before, or indeed which will come after. Here are integuments at last—and Jean has not been content with second-hand clothes, but instead has produced something unique in making a pattern which incorporates both secular and sacred imagery of the most sobering kind. After this, Amant's sexual climax may well appear as something of an anticlimax, his elaborate innuendo trivial and bathetic. Here Jean de Meun is not so much lifting the veil as looking up skirts. In structural terms, he was taking an extraordinary risk. Maybe the *Rose* never recovers from it.⁸⁰

---

⁷⁷ *Le Débat*, ed. Hicks, pp. 94-95; trans. Baird and Kane, p. 98 (alteration added).
⁷⁸ *Le Débat*, ed. Hicks, p. 112; trans. Baird and Kane, p. 115.
⁷⁹ On this comparison see especially P.-Y. Badel, *Le 'Roman de la Rose' au XIVᵉ siècle. Étude de la réception de l'oeuvre* (Geneva, 1980), pp. 486-89.
⁸⁰ That certainly was the view of Christine de Pizan. In replying to the letter from Pierre Col which has been quoted above, she argues that 'a work stands or falls by its conclusion', and Jean de Meun has failed to conclude 'in favour of the moral way of life'. Later she declares that 'he brings paradise into the filthy things that he describes' in order to give greater credibility ('plus foy') to his book, and (in

* * * * *

I'd like to end with reference to an anonymous twelfth-century poem (beginning *Nature talamos intrans reseransque poeta*), which clearly was influenced by the passage from Macrobius which formed my opening citation.[81] Here a poet who had entered the house of Nature, and subsequently dared to reveal her secrets, is castigated. This figure finds himself in a dark wood, threatened by wild beasts. But in a small clearing an old house stands, all by itself, and the poet can discern a naked maiden within. On asking for shelter, he is refused; hiding her nakedness with her hair and hands, the woman accuses him of having broken faith with her: 'Stand afar off, and do no more wrong to my modesty. Only with difficulty did I bring myself to allow you to enter into my mysteries. You ought to have kept perpetual faith. Why, then, have you not been afraid to make me common, and, by spreading abroad what you knew about me, prostituted me, as though I were worthy of the name of a harlot? For this reason I will not suffer you any longer to look closely upon me, but I will cast you out and leave you to death and the beasts'. Here, as F.J.E. Raby puts it, 'that what Nature commands to be

---

contrast to the view of Laurent de Premierfait as quoted above) compares the *Rose* unfavourably with the *Divine Comedy*: 'If you wish to hear paradise and hell described more subtly and, theologically, portrayed more advantageously, poetically, and efficaciously, read the book of Dante [...] I say that you will find there sounder principles [...]' (in *Le Débat*, ed. Hicks, pp. 134-35, 141-42; trans. Baird and Kane, pp. 132, 138). More broadly, Gerson states that Jean de Meun added 'a most shameful conclusion', but also 'an irrational middle in opposition to Reason', to what Guillaume de Lorris had begun; he too believed that the poet had not ultimately condemned vice with the requisite clarity and thoroughness. In *Le Débat*, ed. Hicks, p. 85-86; trans. Baird and Kane, p. 89.

[81] Edited and discussed by Raby, 'Nuda Natura'. As he points out, the poem was almost certainly influenced by Macrobius's anecdote concerning the philosopher Numenius, who 'had revealed to him in a dream the outrage he had committed against the gods by proclaiming his interpretation (*interpretando vulgaverit*) of the Eleusinian mysteries. The Eleusinian goddesses themselves, dressed in the garments of courtesans, appeared to him standing before an open brothel, and when in his astonishment he asked the reason for this shocking conduct, they angrily replied that he had driven them from their sanctuary of modesty and had prostituted them to every passer-by'. (*In somn. Scip.*, I.ii.19; trans. Stahl, p. 87). See further William of Conches's commentary on this Macrobius passage, quoted and discussed by Dronke, *Fabula*, pp. 53-55.

hidden is to be expounded only to the few who are fit to receive it, lest it should become of no account when heard by the vulgar'.[82]

Who was that poet? We may never know (assuming for the moment that a particular individual was being criticized here), but for our purposes he may be identified as someone rather like Jean de Meun. For Jean could be said to have made known the secrets of Nature to the vulgar, and in the vulgar tongue at that. In the *Rose* we see Nature leaving her old house, and taking faltering steps in search of a new audience, an interpretative community wider and more diverse than that presupposed by Alan of Lille. Like W.B. Yeats long after him, Jean was content to leave to others certain 'embroideries / Out of old mythologies', believing that 'there's more enterprise / In walking naked'.[83]

---

[82] Raby, 'Nuda Natura', p. 77.
[83] 'A Coat', in *The Collected Poems of W.B. Yeats* (London, 1965), p. 142.

KING'S COLLEGE LONDON
MEDIEVAL STUDIES

ISSN 0953-217X

General Editor: Janet Bately
Executive Editor: David Hook

I: James E. Cross, *Cambridge Pembroke College MS 25: a Carolingian sermonary used by Anglo-Saxon preachers*. viii + 252 pp., 1987. ISBN 0 9513085 0 5. £9.75.

II: *The Sacred Nectar of the Greeks: the study of Greek in the West in the Early Middle Ages*, edited by Michael W. Herren in collaboration with Shirley Ann Brown. (10) + xii + 313 pp., 24 plates, 1988. ISBN 0 9513085 1 3. £17.00.

III: *Cultures in Contact in Medieval Spain: historical and literary essays presented to L.P. Harvey*, edited by David Hook & Barry Taylor. xvi + 216 pp., 1990. ISBN 0 9513085 2 1. £16.

IV: *Eleven Old English Rogationtide Homilies*, edited by Joyce Bazire and James E. Cross. xxxii + 143 pp., 1989. ISBN 0 9513085 3 X. £9.75.

V: *Chaucer and Fifteenth-century Poetry*, edited by Julia Boffey and Janet Cowen. x + 174 pp., 1991. ISBN 0 9513085 4 8. £9.75.

VI: Lynne Grundy, *Books and Grace: Ælfric's theology*. viii + 290 pp., 1991. ISBN 0 9513085 5 6. £12.

VII: *Richard Coeur de Lion in History and Myth*, edited by Janet L. Nelson. xiv + 165 pp. 1992. ISBN 0 9513085 6 4. £10.50.

VIII: Frank W. Chandler, *A Catalogue of Names of Persons in the German Court Epics. An examination of the literary sources and dissemination together with notes on the etymologies of the more important names*, edited by Martin H. Jones. 1992. ISBN 0 9513085 7 2. £16.50.

IX: *Evangelista's 'Libro de cetrería': a fifteenth-century satire of falconry books*, edited by José Manuel Fradejas Rueda. liv + 87 pp. 1992. ISBN 0 9513085 8 0. £10.50.

X: *Kings and Kingship in Medieval Europe*, edited by Anne J. Duggan. xv + 440 pp., 17 plates, 1993. ISBN 0 9513085 9 9. £20.

XI: Jane Roberts and Christian Kay, with Lynne Grundy, *A Thesaurus of Old English*. 1995. 2 volumes. ISBN 0 9522119 0 4 (complete work).